W9-DEH-414

Sue Graves and Brian Moses

Illustrated by

Tim Archbold

First edition for the United States, its territories and possessions, Canada, the
Philippine Republic, and Puerto Rico published by Barron's Educational Series, Inc., 2001.
Published by arrangement with HarperCollins Publishers Ltd.

First published in 2000 by Collins, a division of HarperCollins Publishers Ltd.

All inquiries should be addressed to:
Barron's Educational Series, Inc.
250 Wireless Blvd.
Hauppauge, NY 11788
www.barronseduc.com

International Standard Book No. 0-7641-1964-8
Library of Congress Catalog Card No.: 2001089445

Acknowledgments:
The authors would like to thank the following for permission to use copyrighted material:
Two lines from "The Mighty Slide" from *The Mighty Slide* by Allan Ahlberg (Viking
Kestrel, 1988) Copyright © Allan Ahlberg 1988.

Every effort has been made to trace copyright holders and to obtain their permission for
the use of copyrighted material. The author and the publishers will gladly receive any
information enabling them to rectify any error or omission in subsequent editions.

Printed in Scotland
9 8 7 6 5 4 3 2 1

Contents

Introduction

What can you do with a rhyming dictionary?

Well, you could use it to help you keep fit.

You could use it to prop up your desk if it's wobbly.

You could sit on it if you can't see the board.

Or you could use it, and this is probably the *best* use, to help you to write your own poems.

plunder, thunder under

dawn, fawn, lawn

yawn

Where do we find rhymes?

Rhymes are all around you and have been from your earliest days. They are an essential part of nursery rhymes:

> Pat-a-cake, pat-a-cake, baker's man,
> Bake me a cake as fast as you can.

They feature in advertisements:

> Forget the rest,
> We're simply the best!

… and playground rhymes:

> Hickory, dickory, dock.
> The mouse ran up the clock.
> The clock struck one,
> The mouse ran down!
> Hickory, dickory, dock.

They appear in greetings cards:

> This birthday wish
> Is just to say
> Have a lovely time
> On your special day.

… and football chants:

> One, two, three, four,
> Who do we want to score?
> J, E, T, S, Jets Jets Jets!

They are used in songs, and in new versions of songs:

> Happy birthday to you,
> Squashed tomatoes and stew,
> Bread and butter in the gutter,
> Happy birthday to you!

Introduction

Can you spot a rhyme?

If you listen to the sound of words then you should be able to spot a rhyme. A rhyme is the repetition of the same sound.

Which three words sound the same in the sentence *The cat sat on the mat*? *Cat, sat* and *mat* all rhyme. Other words that rhyme with *cat, sat* and *mat* are *flat, hat, that, fat* and *splat*! Can you think of some more?

Be careful! A word may have the same spelling pattern and look like it rhymes but it is the sound of the word that is important. For example, the word *what* might look like *that* or *cat* or *hat*, but it doesn't sound like them. *What* sounds more similar to *hot* or *spot*.

Rhymes can be **single rhymes**, where just one sound is repeated as in *cat* and *mat*. They can be **double rhymes**, where two sounds are repeated as in *walking* and *talking*, or even **triple rhymes** as in *teasingly* and *pleasingly*.

In poetry, rhymes can often be found at the end of lines:

> Look at us now, we're stuck up a **tree**,
> Me, my big sister and Kevin who's **three**…

Sometimes rhymes appear in the middle of lines. These are called **internal rhymes**:

> When **Jack** came **back** to school…

What do rhymes do?

Rhymes help to strengthen a poem and make it sound good when read aloud. They add a musical quality to the poem by making the lines "sing."

What are the different types of rhyme?

There are many different types of rhyme. Try using **rhyming couplets** where the first line of a poem rhymes with the second, the third with the fourth, and so on:

> We're stuck up a tree one Sunday in **June**
> hoping that someone comes past very **soon**. ⎤— rhyming couplet
> I bet that we've missed something good on **TV**, ⎤
> I wish that we'd chosen an easier **tree**. ⎦— rhyming couplet

Many poems have rhymes in the second and fourth lines of each verse:

> Spring has come to the city
> to the streets and the railway **line**.
> Winter is packing its bags,
> the sun has begun to **shine**.

Sometimes the rhymes are in the first and third lines of each verse, or even in the first and third *and* the second and fourth. Look out for examples!

A **limerick** is a humorous verse which has five lines and a very strict rhyming pattern. There is a rhyme in the first, second and fifth lines, and a different rhyme in the third and fourth lines:

> There was a young man of **Kildare**
> who bumped into a grizzly **bear**. ⎤ rhyme A
> He had a huge **fright** ⎤ rhyme B
> when the bear hugged him **tight**, ⎦
> so be warned, and of bears please **beware**. ⎦

Introduction

A **tongue twister** is a phrase or a verse that is difficult to say because many of its words have similar sounds. Tongue twisters can be fun to read and to try to write:

How much wood would a woodchuck chuck
If a woodchuck could chuck wood?
He would chuck the wood as much as he could
If a woodchuck could chuck wood.

And then, of course, there's **rapping**. You can have a lot of fun with rapping rhymes!

Matthew, Mark, Luke and **Paul**
drive their teacher up the **wall**.

Mary, Jodie, Faith, **Georgina**
make more noise than a vacuum **cleaner**.

Hip hop **hap**
it's the Class 3 **rap**.

"Activities" on pages 149–159 is full of ideas to help you write your own poetry.

Do the rhymes *feel* right?

When you write your own poem, first decide whether the poem will rhyme or not. I find quite often that when I want to bring humor into a poem, then that poem will probably rhyme. Rhyme works well with humorous verse but isn't always appropriate for more serious poems.

Be tough on yourself with the use of rhyme. It has to work in the poem and it has to work well, otherwise you should look for something else. Sometimes this means changing a line around so that a different word appears at the end of the line, a word that may give you more possibilities for a meaningful rhyme. Meaning is really important, unless it's a nonsense poem.

Try to avoid a silly rhyme, a rhyme that is just there because you simply can't find anything else and you don't want to lose the rhyming pattern.

> At the farm today I saw a **pig**
> I noticed it was wearing a **wig**.

I've lost count of how many times I've seen "pig" and "wig" rhymed in a poem. Predictable rhymes are uninteresting rhymes. Here are two lines by Allan Ahlberg from his poem "The Mighty Slide" which is a wonderful example of a fresh rhyme:

> His wobbly style is **unmistakable**,
> The sign of a boy who knows he's **breakable**.

Do the rhymes help the rhythm?

To help you use rhymes in the right places, begin by following a certain pattern of rhymes, for example, couplets, or second and fourth lines of each verse. Stick with that pattern to make sure that the poem retains its **rhythm**. As you have seen, a regular rhyme will give a poem a definite rhythm.

Introduction

Do the rhymes *sound* right?

Always read your poem again once you have finished it. Read it to yourself to begin with, then read it aloud. Read it to a partner if you can – listen to hear if the rhymes work. Are they natural and unforced?

If you are unhappy with any of the rhymes, work together to find alternatives. You may even decide that the poem would be better without the rhymes, or that some rhymes work better as **near rhymes** rather than exact rhymes, for example, *down* and *around*, *confused* and *barbecues*, *James* and *pain*.

If the rhymes are fine but the lines still don't sound right you could try adding an extra word or taking a word away. In the following line the word *all* isn't needed:

> The night was *all* cold and **dark**
> as I tiptoed through the **park**.

Sometimes what you take out of a poem is just as important as what you put into it. The word *all* adds nothing to the line. The line sounds more dramatic without it.

When you are working on your poem, listen to advice, from your partner, from your teacher, from anyone who is prepared to listen to what you have written.

I always show my poems to my wife because I'm too close to a poem that I've written – I'm too protective of it. I know that she will give me an honest opinion if she feels any of the lines don't work. Sometimes a line that she picks out may be a favorite line of mine. It may be that that particular line is spoiling the poem and I just can't see it. In the end I usually agree that it has to go and that the poem sounds all the better for her advice.

What can you do with the poems you write?

Make your own poetry book. Collect all the poems you have written and present them in a book with an eye-catching cover. Give your book a title: maybe your favorite poem in the collection, or a line that you are pleased with, or a rhyme. You can illustrate your books or swap with a partner and illustrate each other's.

Introduction

Look out for competitions and other places where your poems might stand a chance of being published. Comics, magazines, television programs, local papers and local radio will sometimes hold poetry competitions. Your teacher might be able to tell you about others. Try to enter as many as you can. It is great fun to see something published in the paper or hear it read on the radio.

Read your poems aloud. Hold poetry readings for children in other classes, for your parents or as part of assemblies. Record the poems on tape and swap tapes with other classes.

And a final word (in rhyme of course!)

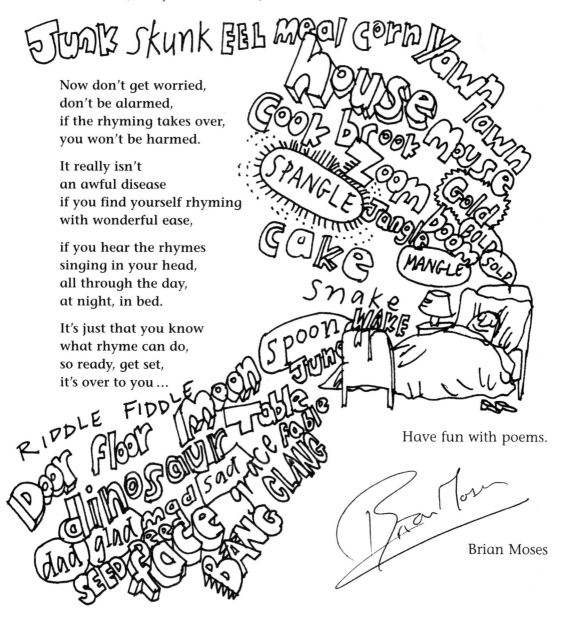

Now don't get worried,
don't be alarmed,
if the rhyming takes over,
you won't be harmed.

It really isn't
an awful disease
if you find yourself rhyming
with wonderful ease,

if you hear the rhymes
singing in your head,
all through the day,
at night, in bed.

It's just that you know
what rhyme can do,
so ready, get set,
it's over to you ...

Have fun with poems.

Brian Moses

How to use this dictionary

Each page of the *Rhyming Dictionary* is similar to the one shown on page 13. The following steps show you how to use this dictionary to find rhyming words.

1. If you know the word you want to find rhymes for, use the A–Z Index starting on page 160. (You can also find the word by skimming through the dictionary using the alphabet line that runs down the edge of each page.) Find the word *hare* under *Hh* in the A–Z Index.

2. If you don't know a word, but you know the sound, use the Rhyming Sounds Index beginning on page 185. Look up the sound *-are* in the Rhyming Sounds Index. You will see that the headword is *hare*. Look up this headword in the main dictionary.

3. Once you have found the word *hare*, look at the boxes of words around it. Each box contains words that rhyme with *hare* – some have the same spelling pattern, some have a different spelling pattern. Any of the words you choose from these boxes will rhyme with *hare*.

4. On some pages, you will find a short poem which uses rhyming words that are listed on that page. If you wish, you could use some of the rhymes used in that poem, use the poem as a model or extend it to create your own version.

Features used in the dictionary

Ⓐ Guide words
Guide words on left-hand pages tell you the first headword to appear on each page. Guide words on right-hand pages tell you the last headword to appear on each page.

Ⓑ Headword
The headword (main word) is in blue. All the words in the word family boxes rhyme with the headword.

Ⓒ Alphabet line
The alphabet line helps you to find your way around the dictionary.

How to use this dictionary

D **Word family box**

The words in a word family box have the same spelling patterns. All the words in the word family boxes rhyme with the headword.

E **Compound words**

You might find compound words in the word family boxes. A compound word is made up of two or more words.

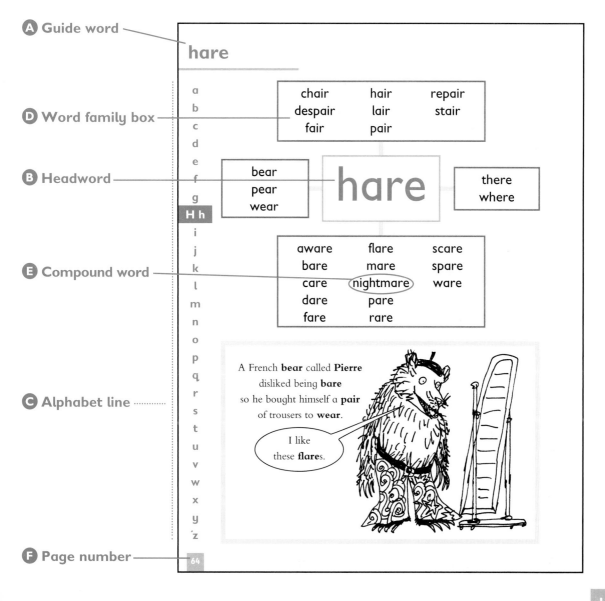

A Guide word

D Word family box

B Headword

E Compound word

C Alphabet line

F Page number

hare

chair	hair	repair
despair	lair	stair
fair	pair	

bear
pear
wear

hare

there
where

aware	flare	scare
bare	mare	spare
care	nightmare	ware
dare	pare	
fare	rare	

A French **bear** called **Pierre** disliked being **bare** so he bought himself a **pair** of trousers to **wear**.

I like these **flare**s.

a b c d e f g H h i j k l m n o p q r s t u v w x y z

64

13

How to use this dictionary

How to use the A–Z Index on page 160

All the words used in the dictionary are listed in alphabetical order in the A–Z Index. The following steps show you how to use this dictionary to find rhyming words for *band*.

1. The word *band* begins with *b* so find the initial letter guide *Bb* in the index.

2. Look at the second letter of the word *band*. Now look down the list until you find the first word beginning with *ba-*. There are a few words that begin with *ba-* so look at the next letter in *band*. Now look down the list until you find words beginning with *ban-* and there you will find *band*.

3. Next to the word *band* is the page number 63. Turn to this page to find words that rhyme with *band*.

Initial letter guides
The initial letter guides will help you to find your way around the index.

Headwords
The words in bold are headwords (main words). Words that rhyme with the headwords can be found on the pages listed.

Page numbers
Look on this page to find the rhyming words.

attack 20	bark 99	before 42
author 56	barred 61	beg 100
aware 64	barrow 18	beginner 140
away 144	base 50	behalf 62
awoke 95	bash 19	beige 30
Bb	bask 87	believe 121
	baste 138	belittle 84
babyish 54	**bat** 22	bell 139
babysitter 26	batch 87	bellow 18
back 20	bate 103	below 18
backpack 20	batter 88	belt 88
bad 39	battleship 147	bend 49
bade 120	bawl 21	bent 126
badger 56	bay 144	**berry** 24
bag 55	beach 111	best 136
bail 91	**beak** 23	bet 137
bait 103	beam 43	beyond 105
baize 26	bean 107	bib 112
bake 31	beanstalk 138	bid 82
bale 91	bear 64	biff 33
ball 21	beast 52	big 41
balloon 89	beat 47	**bike** 24
balm 18	became 92	bile 127
bamboo 148	beck 92	bill 71
ban 136	bed 65	bin 102
band 63	bedtime 128	bind 53
bandage 118	**bee** 23	**bird** 24
bandit 25	beech 111	birch 101
bang 22	beef 112	**bit** 25
bangle 16	beehive 41	bite 81
bank 124	been 107	**bitter** 26
bap 86	beep-beep 37	black 20
bar 74	beer 46	blackberry 24
barbecue 108	bees 32	blackcurrant 17
bare 64	beet 47	blame 92

How to use this dictionary

How to use the Rhyming Sounds Index on page 185

The Rhyming Sounds Index will help you to find words that rhyme with one another. The following steps explain how to use this index to find rhyming words for the sound -*ail*.

1. Find the **sound**. Decide which sound you want to find a rhyming word for, e.g. -*ail*. Look up this sound in the sound column. The sounds are listed alphabetically, so look for sounds beginning with *ail*.

2. Find the **headword**. Look at the headword which is in the column next to the sound. The headword in this case is *nail*.

3. Find the **page number**. The page on which you will find the headword is in the next column.

4. **More rhyming sounds**. In the last column next to the page number you will find more sounds which rhyme with the headword, but which are spelled differently. You can find these rhyming sounds on the same page as the headword.

   Turn to page 91 to find more words that rhyme with *nail*.

sound	headword	page number	more rhyming sounds
-able	table	124	-abel
-ace	face	50	-aice, -ase
-ach	match	87	-atch
-ack	back	20	-ac, -ak
-ad	dad	39	add
-ade	shade	120	-aid, -ayed, -eyed
-aft	raft	110	-aughed, -aught
-ag	flag	55	
-age	cage	30	-eige
-ail	nail	91	-ale, -eil

Sound
This is the sound that all the words listed under the headword say.

Headword
The headword introduces a series of word families which all rhyme with each other.

Page number
This tells you on which page you will find the headword and all the word families that rhyme with it.

More rhyming sounds
These sounds rhyme with the sounds in the sound column but they are spelled differently, for example *table* and *label* rhyme but have different spelling patterns.

angle

bangle	mangle	tangle
dangle	spangle	triangle
jangle	strangle	wrangle

jingle-jangle

Look at the **bangle** on my wrist,
see it shine from every **angle**.
Watch it **dangle** from my wrist
and hear it **jingle-jangle**.

ant

chant	grant	rant
decant	pant	scant

ape

cape	grape	shape
drape	nape	shipshape
escape	scrape	tape

arch

larch	parch
march	starch

A a
b
c
d
e
f
g
h
i
j
k
l
m
n
o
p
q
r
s
t
u
v
w
x
y
z

arm

alarm	harm
charm	underarm
farm	

bellow	buffalo	mosquito
fellow	domino	no
mellow	echo	radio
yellow		

hoe
tiptoe
toe

sew

arrow

although
though

oh

hello

below	know	scarecrow	wallow
blow	mow	shadow	wheelbarrow
borrow	narrow	show	
crow	pillow	tomorrow	

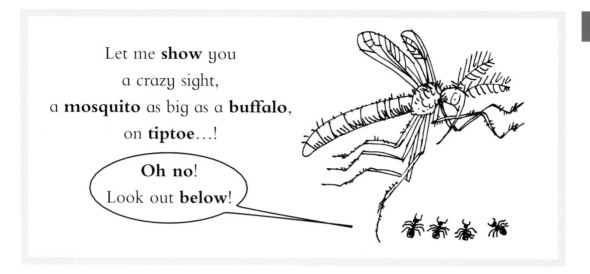

Let me **show** you
a crazy sight,
a **mosquito** as big as a **buffalo**,
on **tiptoe**…!

Oh no!
Look out **below**!

art

cart	dart	go-cart	smart
chart	depart	part	tart

ash

bash	flash	mash	smash
crash	gnash	mishmash	splash
dash	lash	rash	trash

a
B b
c
d
e
f
g
h
i
j
k
l
m
n
o
p
q
r
s
t
u
v
w
x
y
z

Bb

| cul-de-sac | **back** | anorak |

attack	lack	snack
backpack	pack	stack
black	quack	track
crack	rack	whack
hack	sack	
haystack	smack	

bawl
brawl
crawl

ball

maul

call	hall	tall
fall	mall	wall
football	stall	

A soccer player named **Paul**
found he couldn't control the **ball**.
He tried very hard
each night in his yard
but the **ball** just flew over the **wall**.

Can I
have my **ball** back,
please?

a
B b
c
d
e
f
g
h
i
j
k
l
m
n
o
p
q
r
s
t
u
v
w
x
y
z

bang

clang	hang	rang
fang	overhang	sang
gang	pang	

See the crazy **cat**
as he tries to catch
a passing **bat**.
See him leap and then
splat!
That **cat** is no **acrobat**!

bat

acrobat	fat	mat	sat
brat	gnat	pat	splat
cat	hat	rat	that

beak

antique

creak	peak	creek	peek
freak	squeak	leek	seek
leak	weak	meek	week

chimpanzee	see	chimney
free	three	key
knee	tree	monkey

bee

pea	he she
sea	me we

simile

ski

army   happy
chemistry

A **bee** said to a **chimpanzee**
as they sat together in a **tree**:
"Don't you **monkey** around with **me**!"

berry

necessary

berry

very

bury

blackberry   cherry   merry
blueberry   ferry   strawberry

bike

hike   pike   strike
motorbike   spike   trike

third

heard

bird

herd

curd

stirred
whirred

crossword
word

bit

fidget
trumpet

bandit	kit	slit
exit	knit	spit
fit	nitwit	split
flit	pit	twit
hit	sit	wit

Turn "**split**" into "**slit**,"
no "p."
Turn "**split**" into "**spit**,"
no "l."
Noel?
Merry Christmas.

a
B b
c
d
e
f
g
h
i
j
k
l
m
n
o
p
q
r
s
t
u
v
w
x
y
z

bitter

babysitter	jitter	spitter
fitter	knitter	titter
glitter	litter	
hitter	sitter	

| amaze | gaze | haze |
| craze | graze | maze |

maize

blaze

phase
phrase

brays	lays	rays
days	pays	stays
delays	prays	sways

boat

afloat   gloat
coat   moat
float   overcoat
goat   throat

note   vote
quote   wrote

A strange **note**
came
from the **throat**
of a **goat**
afloat
in a **boat**:
I **quote**…

Help!

a

B b

c

d

e

f

g

h

i

j

k

l

m

n

o

p

q

r

s

t

u

v

w

x

y

z

bolt

colt   revolt

jolt   volt

boy

ahoy   coy   ploy

annoy   enjoy   toy

| antic | elastic | heroic | music | picnic |
| arithmetic | frantic | magic | panic | |

brick

chick	kick	lipstick	sick	tick
crick	lick	pick	stick	trick
flick	limerick	quick	thick	wick

A **limerick** writer from **Wick**
found the **limerick**s making him **sick**.
"I'm up half the night
and they still won't go right,
I must **quick**ly **kick** this habit."

No, I must **kick** this habit, and **quick**...ly. Oh, **pick** what you like!

bubble

| rubble stubble |

| double trouble |

a
b
C c
d
e
f
g
h
i
j
k
l
m
n
o
p
q
r
s
t
u
v
w
x
y
z

Cc

cage

age	rage	wage
enrage	sage	
page	stage	

beige

break steak	opaque	ache headache

cake

bake	flake	mistake	sake	stake
brake	lake	pancake	snake	take
fake	make	rake	snowflake	wake

You might **make** a **mistake**
if you tried to **wake** a **snake**
    to feed him a **cake**.

Not me,
you'll get a stomach
ache.

a
b
C c
d
e
f
g
h
i
j
k
l
m
n
o
p
q
r
s
t
u
v
w
x
y
z

fleas
peas

these

breeze
sneeze

cheese

displease
please
tease

keys

bees
knees
trees

chop

flop   mop   stop
hop   plop   top
lollipop   pop

swap

cliff

if

biff   skiff   tiff
miff   sniff   whiff
sheriff   stiff

clown

down	town
drown	upside-down
frown	

| noun |
| pronoun |

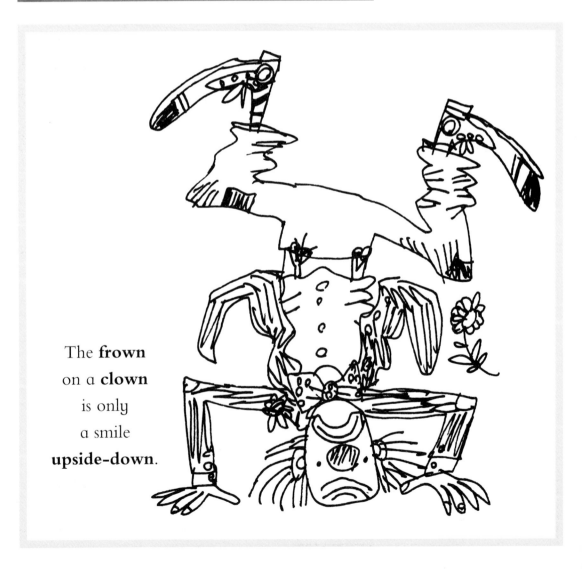

The **frown**
on a **clown**
is only
a smile
upside-down.

coast

boast	toast
roast	

ghost	most
host	post
lamppost	

goad	road
load	toad

code

crowed	sowed
flowed	stowed
owed	towed
rowed	

abode	rode
explode	strode
ode	zip code

a
b
C c
d
e
f
g
h
i
j
k
l
m
n
o
p
q
r
s
t
u
v
w
x
y
z

rolled
strolled

cold

bowled

blindfold	fold	hold	told
bold	gold	sold	unfold

count

amount	discount	mount

COW

allow	bow	how	pow	vow
anyhow	eyebrow	now	sow	wow

creep

beep	oversleep	sleep
deep	peep	steep
jeep	seep	sweep
keep	sheep	weep

heap
leap
reap

At the edge of the lane
a dozy **sheep**,
just woken up from a very **deep sleep**,
was forced to **leap**
when a speeding **jeep**
tore past her.

Beep-beep!

crisp

lisp   will-o'-the-wisp   wisp

cross

boss   gloss   moss
floss   loss   toss

crust

bust   gust   rust
distrust   just   trust
dust   must

bussed
fussed

Dd

dad

bad	had	mad
fad	kneepad	pad
glad	lad	sad

add

dance

a
b
c
D d
e
f
g
h
i
j
k
l
m
n
o
p
q
r
s
t
u
v
w
x
y
z

dance

advance	glance	stance
chance	lance	trance
France	prance	

Hi! I'm Jo
and I love to **dance**.
Around the house
I spin and **prance**.
Just look at me
I'm in a **trance**.
My name's Jo
and I love to **dance**.

dig

big	fig	pig	sprig	wig
earwig	jig	rig	twig	

dive

I've

alive	beehive	drive	hive	live
arrive	chive	five	jive	strive

dog

bog	fog	log
catalog	frog	slog
cog	hedgehog	smog
flog	jog	

dialogue

41

door

before
bore
more
score
sore
store

four
your

for
nor

door

boar
roar

floor
moor

dinosaur

Don't open the **door**
if you hear a **ROAR**
or see a big **claw**,
it may well be
a **dinosaur**...

Shut that
door!

dove

above	love
glove	shove

deem	scheme
seem	theme

dream

beam	scream	stream	team
cream	steam	sunbeam	

a
b
c
D d
e
f
g
h
i
j
k
l
m
n
o
p
q
r
s
t
u
v
w
x
y
z

drink

brink	mink	think
chink	pink	tiddlywink
ink	rink	wink
link	sink	

If your horrid little brother
offers you a **drink**,
just **think**
before you **drink**,
it could be **ink**!

crumb	numb
dumb	thumb

come	# drum	kingdom

chum	pendulum	strum
gum	plum	sum
hum	rum	yum-yum

a
b
c
d
E e
f
g
h
i
j
k
l
m
n
o
p
q
r
s
t
u
v
w
x
y
z

E e

beer	jeer
cheer	peer
deer	steer

here
mere

ear

pier

appear	fear	rear
clear	gear	spear
dear	hear	tear
disappear	near	year

beet	meet
feet	sweet

eat

delete

beat	heat	repeat
cheat	meat	seat
defeat	neat	treat
feat	peat	wheat

Pete's mom said she knew a **neat** way to **beat** the problem **Pete** had with his smelly **feet**.

Now they really smell **sweet**!

a
b
c
d
E e
f
g
h
i
j
k
l
m
n
o
p
q
r
s
t
u
v
w
x
y
z

edge

dredge	ledge	wedge
fledge	pledge	
hedge	sledge	

allege

eel

feel	peel
heel	reel
keel	steel
kneel	wheel

appeal	real
deal	squeal
heal	steal
ideal	veal
meal	

A plate of steamed **eel** is not my idea of an **ideal meal** – ugh!

I'd **squeal**!

elf

herself	itself	shelf
himself	self	yourself

end

bend	intend	send
blend	lend	tend
defend	mend	trend
extend	pretend	
friend	rend	

a
b
c
d
e
F f
g
h
i
j
k
l
m
n
o
p
q
r
s
t
u
v
w
x
y
z

Ff

base	case
bookcase	

face

brace	pace	space
grace	place	trace
lace	race	
misplace	replace	

fairy

airy   hairy
dairy

canary   vary
dictionary   wary
scary

When a bad-tempered **fairy** flew out of **Mary**'s **dictionary**, it was **scary**!

In the future, I'll be **wary**.

fashion

passion
ration

feast

beast	least
east	yeast

creased	released
greased	

fence

consequence	dense	sense
hence	nonsense	tense

find

bind	mind
blind	rind
grind	unwind
hind	wind

fined	pined
lined	signed
mined	

a
b
c
d
e
F f
g
h
i
j
k
l
m
n
o
p
q
r
s
t
u
v
w
x
y
z

burst   outburst

worst

first

thirst

cursed   nursed   pursed

fish

dish	shellfish	wish
jellyfish	squish	
selfish	swish	

Jellyfish,
jellyfish,
odd and funny-looking
umbrellyfish,
slimy old seaside smellyfish.
Jellyfish,
jellyfish.

flag

bag	gag	stag
brag	handbag	teabag
crag	rag	wag
drag	sag	

flower

devour	our
flour	sour
hour	

cauliflower	power
cower	tower

fur

a
b
c
d
e
F f
g
h
i
j
k
l
m
n
o
p
q
r
s
t
u
v
w
x
y
z

author
calculator

blur

purr

fur

were

whirr

fir   sir   stir

badger   otter
her   shimmer

See something **stir**,
　a **blur** of **fur**,
　　a **purr**,
　　　It's a…

Gg

giggle

jiggle	wiggle
squiggle	wriggle

girl

earl   pearl

girl

curl hurl	swirl whirl
furl uncurl	twirl

Watch the dancer
whirl and **twirl**,
curl and **uncurl**,
what a **girl**!

glass

brass	grass	pass
class	outclass	trespass

globe

disrobe	probe
lobe	robe

grease

a
b
c
d
e
f

G g

h
i
j
k
l
m
n
o
p
q
r
s
t
u
v
w
x
y
z

lease
release

peace

police

grease

fleece

mantelpiece   piece
niece

foul

growl

towel
trowel

fowl   jowl   scowl
howl   prowl   waterfowl

grunt

blunt	runt
hunt	shunt
punt	stunt

confront   front

Don't stand up at the **front** of a boat, it might prove to be a silly **stunt**.

bodyguard

guard

barred	marred
jarred	starred

card	lard
farmyard	yard
hard	

a b c d e f **G g** h i j k l m n o p q r s t u v w x y z

a
b
c
d
e
f
g
H h
i
j
k
l
m
n
o
p
q
r
s
t
u
v
w
x
y
z

Hh

| behalf |
| calf |

half

| giraffe |

| laugh |

A **giraffe**
in a long scarf,
what a **laugh**!

hand

band	land
brand	sand
grand	strand
handstand	understand

canned	planned
fanned	tanned

handle

candle	manhandle

sandal	vandal
scandal	

hare

a b c d e f g

H h

i j k l m n o p q r s t u v w x y z

chair	hair	repair
despair	lair	stair
fair	pair	

bear		there
pear	**hare**	where
wear		

aware	flare	scare
bare	mare	spare
care	nightmare	ware
dare	pare	
fare	rare	

A French **bear** called **Pierre**
disliked being **bare**
so he bought himself a **pair**
of trousers to **wear**.

I like these **flare**s.

head

said

bread   sleepyhead
instead   spread
lead   thread
read   tread

bed   red
bled   shred
fed   wed
led

health

commonwealth   wealth
stealth

hinge

cringe   syringe
singe   tinge

| comb |
| honeycomb |

home

| chrome | gnome |
| dome | tome |

| foam | roam |
| loam | |

| could | would |
| should | |

hood

good	stood
misunderstood	understood
neighborhood	wood

hook

book	cookbook	overtook
brook	look	unhook
cook	nook	

A **cook** had to **look**
In his recipe **book**
When he **mistook**
The time it **took**
For the dish to **cook**.

Don't **overcook** it this time!

hope

antelope   mope   rope
cope   pope

soap

---

coarse
hoarse

course
source

horse

divorce   force
enforce

house

clubhouse   louse   warehouse
doghouse   madhouse
lighthouse   mouse

This **house** is making me mad,
said a **mouse**,
this **house** is making me spin.
There are too many steps
in this **lighthouse**,
I get dizzy each time I go in.

hutch

clutch   double Dutch   much   such

a
b
c
d
e
f
g
h
I i
j
k
l
m
n
o
p
q
r
s
t
u
v
w
x
y
z

ice

advice	mice	slice
dice	nice	spice
entice	price	twice
lice	rice	

paradise

Nice!

A split sack of **rice**
is **paradise**
for two fat **mice**.

daffodil   nostril
nil   until

ill

bill	hill	still
chill	kill	swill
dill	mill	till
fill	pill	uphill
frill	quill	will
gill	shrill	
grill	spill	

inch

clinch	flinch	winch
finch	pinch	

a
b
c
d
e
f
g
h
I i
j
k
l
m
n
o
p
q
r
s
t
u
v
w
x
y
z

insect

collect	elect	neglect
correct	expect	protect
disinfect	infect	subject
eject	inspect	

enrich	rich
ostrich	which

itch

ditch	snitch	twitch
hitch	stitch	witch
pitch	switch	

Jj

lamb

jam

am	ram	tram
dam	scram	wham
gram	slam	
ham	swam	

scram

jar

are

jar

bar	guitar	star
car	scar	tar
far	spar	

See the **star**
in his big fast **car**,
playing **guitar**,
he'll go **far**…

Wait!

judge

budge	misjudge	smudge
fudge	nudge	trudge
grudge	sludge	

jug

ugh

bug	humbug	shrug
chug	mug	smug
dug	plug	tug
hug	rug	

a
b
c
d
e
f
g
h
i
J j
k
l
m
n
o
p
q
r
s
t
u
v
w
x
y
z

jumble

bumble	mumble
crumble	rough-and-tumble
fumble	rumble
grumble	stumble
humble	tumble

jump

bump	lump
crump	plump
dump	pump
frump	rump
high jump	stump
hump	sump

junk

bunk	dunk	skunk
chipmunk	hunk	sunk
chunk	punk	trunk

monk

I saw the ghost of a **monk** as it **slunk** past the **trunk** of a tree…

But it didn't see me…

a
b
c
d
e
f
g
h
i
j
K k
l
m
n
o
p
q
r
s
t
u
v
w
x
y
z

K k

kernel

| colonel | journal |

---

kettle

| settle   unsettle | metal   petal |

kilt

hilt	silt	wilt
jilt	stilt	
lilt	tilt	

built	quilt
guilt	rebuilt

The cupboard that Angus **built**
in which to keep his **kilt**,
developed a serious **tilt**
and had to be **rebuilt**.

a
b
c
d
e
f
g
h
i
j

K k

l
m
n
o
p
q
r
s
t
u
v
w
x
y
z

king

brainstorming	ping	spring
bring	ring	sting
building	sing	swing
ceiling	sling	thing
nothing	something	wing

cowardice

kiss

this

amiss	dismiss	miss
bliss	hiss	Swiss

A **kiss** in the dark
may be **bliss**,
unless of course
you **miss**!

bright	knight	might	right	tonight
fight	light	moonlight	sight	
headlight	midnight	plight	tight	

height

kite

bite	mite	quite	white
excite	polite	spite	write

A **polite knight**
said it wouldn't be **right**
to cancel his **midnight fight**
even though he'd turned **quite white**
at the thought of his **plight**.

knuckle

buckle	honeysuckle	unbuckle
chuckle	suckle	

a
b
c
d
e
f
g
h
i
j
K k
l
m
n
o
p
q
r
s
t
u
v
w
x
y
z

a
b
c
d
e
f
g
h
i
j
k
L l
m
n
o
p
q
r
s
t
u
v
w
x
y
z

lamp

amp	clamp	ramp	tramp
camp	cramp	scamp	
champ	damp	stamp	

lid

naked

bid	forbid	kid	slid
did	grid	pyramid	stupid
eyelid	hid	skid	undid

| antonym |
| gym |

limb

| hymn |

| brim | grim | prim | slim | trim |
| dim | him | rim | swim | whim |

Tim joined a **gym**
on a **whim**,
to **swim**
and keep **trim**.

This is **grim**.

limp

chimp	scrimp	wimp
crimp	shrimp	
primp	skimp	

little

belittle	skittle	whittle
brittle	spittle	

lock

block	dock	knock	stock
chock	flock	rock	tick-tock
clock	frock	shock	unlock
crock	hock	sock	

loft

coughed

scoffed

hayloft	soft	waft

poured   toured

roared   soared

lord

ward

afford   cord
chord   sword

board   overboard
hoard

The dragon **roared**
when a Knight with a **sword**
stole his treasure **hoard**.

Quick, bring it
on **board**.

tongue

lung

young

dung   hung   sprung   sung
flung   rung   stung   wrung

a
b
c
d
e
f
g
h
i
j
k
Ll
m
n
o
p
q
r
s
t
u
v
w
x
y
z

a
b
c
d
e
f
g
h
i
j
k
l
M m
n
o
p
q
r
s
t
u
v
w
x
y
z

Mm

map

cap	kidnap	rap	strap	wrap
chap	lap	sap	tap	yap
flap	nap	scrap	thunderclap	zap
gap	overlap	slap	trap	

Biff, bang, wallop and **slap**,
we'll **zap** you loud as a **thunderclap**,
we know your feet will really **tap**
when you hear our noisy family **rap**.

mask

ask   cask   task
bask   flask   unmask

mast

classed
passed

blast   forecast   vast
cast   last
fast   past

match

batch   hatch   scratch
catch   latch   thatch
dispatch   patch

attach

a
b
c
d
e
f
g
h
i
j
k
l
M m
n
o
p
q
r
s
t
u
v
w
x
y
z

matter

batter	flatter	patter
chatter	latter	pitter-patter
fatter	natter	splatter

Fish in **batter**
makes you **fatter**!

melt

belt	knelt	unbelt
felt	pelt	welt
heartfelt	smelt	

dealt

mint

footprint   print   tint
hint   sprint
lint   squint

mob

bob   doorknob   knob   rob
cob   job   lob   sob

moon

strewn

June
prune

afternoon   noon   swoon
balloon   soon
boon   spoon

a
b
c
d
e
f
g
h
i
j
k
l
M m
n
o
p
q
r
s
t
u
v
w
x
y
z

a
b
c
d
e
f
g
h
i
j
k
l
M m
n
o
p
q
r
s
t
u
v
w
x
y
z

mother

another grandmother smother
brother other

Oh **brother** of mine
you must have had
another mother.
No **mother** of mine
would have given birth
to a **brother** like you!

Pull the
other one.

mud

blood
flood

bud rosebud
cud stud
dud thud

| ale | gale | sale | stale | whale |
| dale | pale | scale | tale | |

veil

ail	fingernail	mail	sail	wail
bail	hail	pail	snail	
fail	jail	rail	tail	

Someone sat on **Abigail**'s **snail**,
her face turned **pale**,
it made her **wail**,
but the **snail** survived –
what a **tale**!

Sorry!

a
b
c
d
e
f
g
h
i
j
k
l
m
N n
o
p
q
r
s
t
u
v
w
x
y
z

name

became	fame	lame
blame	flame	nickname
came	frame	same
dame	game	shame

aim
claim

neck

beck	fleck	speck
check	peck	wreck
deck	shipwreck	

discotheque

next

| context   text | flexed   vexed |

nibble

| dribble   scribble
quibble | impossible   possible |

a
b
c
d
e
f
g
h
i
j
k
l
m
N n
o
p
q
r
s
t
u
v
w
x
y
z

universe
verse

worse

nurse

rehearse

curse
purse

Is there any **worse verse** in the whole **universe**?

A pig in a wig danced a jig

nut

putt

but	gut	jut	smut
cut	haircut	rut	strut
doughnut	hut	shut	

Oo

folk		cloak
yolk	**oak**	croak
		soak

awoke	coke	smoke	woke
broke	joke	stroke	yoke
choke	poke	sunstroke	

oblong

along	gong	prong	strong
bong	long	singsong	tong
dong	ping-pong	song	wrong

ocean

commotion	lotion	potion
emotion	motion	
locomotion	notion	

What a **commotion**
at the bottom of the **ocean**
when a squid had a **notion**
to set himself in **motion**!

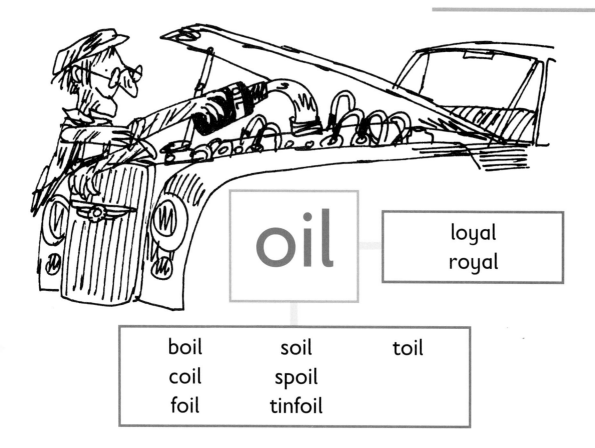

oil

loyal
royal

boil	soil	toil
coil	spoil	
foil	tinfoil	

grandson	ton
son	won

one

bun	pun
fun	run
gun	sun

anyone	none
done	undone
everyone	well-done

a
b
c
d
e
f
g
h
i
j
k
l
m
n
O o
p
q
r
s
t
u
v
w
x
y
z

97

out

b
c
d
e
f
g
h
i
j
k
l
m
n
O o
p
q
r
s
t
u
v
w
x
y
z

doubt

drought

out

about	gout	shout
bout	pout	sprout
clout	roundabout	stout

Did you see the boy **scout**
on the **roundabout**,
as it whirled **about**
too quickly?

Did you hear him **shout**
"Let me **out**!"?
There's no **doubt**
that he must have felt sickly!

Let me **out**!

98

paint

complaint	quaint	taint
faint	saint	

park

bark	lark	spark
hark	mark	
landmark	shark	

Pirate **Peg**
lost her **leg**
when a **keg** that she rolled
went out of control.

Don't call me
Peg Leg!

egg	# peg

| beg | dreg | keg | leg | nutmeg |

pen

| amen | gentlemen | men | then | wren |
| den | hen | ten | when | |

church
lurch

perch

birch

research
search

die
lie
tie

dye
eye

high
sigh
sky-high

I

pie

hi

dragonfly   shy   sty
fly   sky   try
my   sly   why
nearby   spy

pin

a
b
c
d
e
f
g
h
i
j
k
l
m
n
o
P p
q
r
s
t
u
v
w
x
y
z

| inn | **pin** | examine |

bin	dustbin	kin	thin
chin	fin	robin	tin
din	grin	shin	twin
dolphin	in	sin	win

Have you seen
a **dolphin grin**
as he waggles
his **fin**?

The water's lovely.
Come on **in**!

| **pipe** | type |

| gripe | stripe | windpipe |
| ripe | tripe | wipe |

| bait | wait | | eight | weight |

| straight |

plate

ate	create	hate
classmate	date	mate
communicate	fascinate	slate
congratulate	fate	state
cooperate	gate	

He arranged to meet **Kate**
at **five** to **eight**,
but she had a long **wait**
and she told him **straight**
it would be their last **date**.

We just don't
communicate.

a
b
c
d
e
f
g
h
i
j
k
l
m
n
o
P p
q
r
s
t
u
v
w
x
y
z

point

anoint   disappoint
appoint   joint

roll   stroll

foal   goal

bowl

pole

soul

dole   mole   stole
flagpole   role   tadpole
hole   sole   whole

Did you see that **mole**
do a forward **roll**
into his **hole**?

Is that your
goal?

pond

wand

beyond   bond
blonde   fond

pounce

announce   flounce   pronounce
bounce   ounce

prickle

| fickle | sickle | trickle |
| pickle | tickle | |

nickel

punch

brunch	hunch	scrunch
bunch	lunch	
crunch	munch	

a
b
c
d
e
f
g
h
i
j
k
l
m
n
o
p
Q q
r
s
t
u
v
w
x
y
z

Qq

quarter

daughter slaughter granddaughter	breakwater water

magazine   sardine   trampoline

queen

been keen seen green screen teen	bean dean mean clean lean wean

a
b
c
d
e
f
g
h
i
j
k
l
m
n
o
p
Q q
r
s
t
u
v
w
x
y
z

quiet

diet   disquiet   riot

quiver

| deliver | liver | shiver |
| giver | river | sliver |

| showbiz | # quiz | his |

| fizz | whizz |
| frizz | |

Rr

raft

laughed

aircraft	daft
aft	draft
craft	handicraft

reach

beach	overreach	beech	screech
bleach	peach	breech	speech
each	teach	leech	

See the hot sun **bleach** the **beach** while seagulls **screech** overhead, keeping out of **reach**.

a
b
c
d
e
f
g
h
i
j
k
l
m
n
o
p
q
R r
s
t
u
v
w
x
y
z

| leaf sheaf | **reef** | beef |

| chief   handkerchief grief   thief |

rib

| ad-lib   crib   nib bib   fib   squib |

riddle

| diddle   middle fiddle   twiddle |

collide   side   wide
guide   stride
hide   tide

I'd

ride

dyed
eyed

defied   dried   satisfied
denied   justified   tied
died   lied

I'm sorry I'm late for school, Miss **Stride**,
I was **rid**ing by the River **Clyde**
and a **one-eyed** monster
tied me up, then I escaped
and had to **hide**…
So I'm sorry I'm late for school,
Miss **Stride**.

wad

rod

odd

clod	nod	shod
cod	pod	trod
god	ramrod	

roof

aloof	goof	proof
foolproof	hoof	

toot!

root

fruit

boot	scoot
hoot	shoot
loot	toot

brute	lute
flute	pollute

goes   toes
hoes

chose   pose
hose

doze

rose

sews

flamingos

arrows	flows	rows
blows	knows	snows
bows	lows	sows
crows	rainbows	tows

a
b
c
d
e
f
g
h
i
j
k
l
m
n
o
p
q
R r
s
t
u
v
w
x
y
z

Do **flamingos**
get aching **toes**
as they **pose** on one leg
while they **doze**?

Who **knows**?

rough

enough
tough

buff   fluff   handcuff   muff   scruff
cuff   gruff   huff   puff   stuff

crowned   drowned   frowned

round

bloodhound   hound   sound
bound   mound   underground
found   playground   wound
ground   pound

Ace Detective **Mound** thought his **bloodhound** had **found** an important clue **underground** but when he saw what it was how he **frowned**.

I **found** it in the **ground**.

S s

dragon

salmon

bun	pun	stun
fun	run	
nun	sun	

done

a
b
c
d
e
f
g
h
i
j
k
l
m
n
o
p
q
r
S s
t
u
v
w
x
y
z

bridge	ridge
fridge	smidge

language

sausage

advantage	hostage	postage
bandage	package	
encourage	passage	

rule

school

cool	pool	toadstool
fool	stool	tool

centipede   stampede

he'd
she'd
we'd

seed

lead
mislead
read

bleed	feed	reed
breed	heed	speed
deed	need	weed

A **centipede** wanted to travel
at twice his normal **speed**:
"I **need** to get there first," he said,
"There's sure to be a **stampede**."

a
b
c
d
e
f
g
h
i
j
k
l
m
n
o
p
q
r
S s
t
u
v
w
x
y
z

afraid	paid
laid	raid
mermaid	

| played | strayed |
| prayed | |

shade

obeyed

ade	made	trade
fade	marmalade	wade
glade	spade	

persuade

A **mermaid played** sweet music
while waiting in the **shade**
to **persuade** a lonely sailor
that he shouldn't be **afraid**.

We were **made** for
each other.

a
b
c
d
e
f
g
h
i
j
k
l
m
n
o
p
q
r
S s
t
u
v
w
x
y
z

blurt	hurt
curt	

shirt

expert

dirt	skirt
flirt	squirt

heave	weave
leave	

eve

sleeve

deceive

achieve	grieve
believe	thieve

sport

airport	import	short
export	port	sort
fort	retort	

spot

yacht

squat
swat
what

blot	hot	rot
cot	knot	tot
dot	lot	trot
forgot	not	
got	pot	

troupe

group   soup

swoop

coop   loop   stoop
droop   loop-the-loop   troop
hoop   snoop

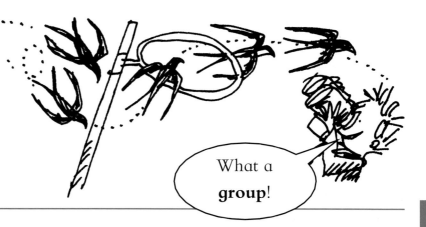

See a **group**
of swallows
loop-the-loop
then **swoop**
through a **hoop**.

What a
group!

syrup

buttercup   hiccup   pup
cup   make-up   sup

table

label

able	fable	stable	turntable
cable	sable	timetable	

tank

bank	plank	sank
flank	prank	stank
gangplank	rank	thank

sewn

bone
cone
microphone
ozone
throne
zone

telephone

blown
grown
known
own
sown
thrown

groan
loan
moan

A visitor from space
was heard to **groan**
when he found he'd parked
by a traffic **cone**
in a no parking **zone**.

I wish
I'd **known**.

NO PARKING

meant

tent

accident	excellent	sent
bent	lent	spent
contentment	rent	vent
dent	scent	went

A goat left a **dent** in my **tent**
and I thought it was an **accident**,
but when he started to chew it,
I knew that he'd **meant** to do it.

Huh,
time I **went**!

thrush

brush	lush	rush
flush	mush	slush
gush	paintbrush	

denial	trial
dial	

style

tile

isle

I'll

bile	pile
file	smile
mile	while

time

rhyme

climb	# time	I'm

bedtime	mime
crime	overtime
dime	slime
lifetime	sublime

Jane took a **train** to **Spain**.
It would have been quicker
to go by **plane**,
but **Jane** gets sick on **plane**s –
what a **pain**!

cane	mane	plane	wane
lane	pane	sane	

rein

train

reign

again	explain	pain	stain
brain	gain	rain	
drain	main	Spain	

truck

buck	luck	suck
chuck	muck	yuck
cluck	pluck	
duck	struck	
dumbstruck	stuck	

tub

club	hub	rub
dub	hubbub	snub
grub	pub	

fern   stern

turn

burn   return
churn   urn

earn   yearn
learn

tusk

mollusk

dusk   husk   musk

a
b
c
d
e
f
g
h
i
j
k
l
m
n
o
p
q
r
s
T t
u
v
w
x
y
z

twist

| fist   list | dismissed   kissed |
| gist | hissed   missed |

My sister's boyfriend said
that he'd **kissed** her,
but I saw her **twist** her head
so he **missed** her.

I think that soon he'll be **dismissed**,
crossed off her **list**!

Uu

under

plunder	thunder	wonder

undress — yes

address	dress	mess
bless	guess	press
chess	happiness	princess
depress	less	stress

a
b
c
d
e
f
g
h
i
j
k
l
m
n
o
p
q
r
s
t
Uu
v
w
x
y
z

a
b
c
d
e
f
g
h
i
j
k
l
m
n
o
p
q
r
s
t
U u
v
w
x
y
z

uniform

lukewarm
swarm
warm

deform   perform
form   storm
inform   thunderstorm

Us, at the back of a **bus**,
big **fuss**!
But **us**, at the front,
top deck,
no **fuss**,
marvelous!

discuss
fuss

us

famous
marvelous

bus   minus
crocus   plus
hippopotamus   thesaurus

abuse   amuse   refuse
accuse   fuse

views

use

ewes

cues   hues

news   stews
pews

These **stews** do not **amuse**!

Use carrots!

I **refuse**.

a
b
c
d
e
f
g
h
i
j
k
l
m
n
o
p
q
r
s
t
u
V v
w
x
y
z

Vv

van

ban	man	ran	tan
bran	milkman	saucepan	than
fan	pan	scan	

vest

best	jest	pest	test
chest	lest	rest	west
guest	nest	suggest	

guessed
messed

debt	**vet**	sweat

alphabet	fret	jet	net	wet
bet	get	let	pet	yet
forget	internet	met	set	

Come on, **let**'s **get** surfing,
surfing the **internet**.
How wonderful to go surfing
and never have to **get wet**.

Hmm, I **bet**!

How to become
a vet
Buying a pet
www.

a
b
c
d
e
f
g
h
i
j
k
l
m
n
o
p
q
r
s
t
u
v
W w
x
y
z

waist

chased

baste	taste
haste	waste

paced	spaced
raced	traced
shamefaced	

walk

hawk
squawk

beanstalk	stalk
chalk	talk

well

expel
gel
rebel

bell	fell	smell
cell	hell	tell
dell	quell	yell
dwell	sell	
farewell	shell	

The **hotel** that **Belle** stayed in
had a most peculiar **smell**.
Nobody could **tell** her what it was
so **Belle** quickly said **farewell**.

I'm **well** out
of there.

NEVERDWELL
HOTEL

Belle

a
b
c
d
e
f
g
h
i
j
k
l
m
n
o
p
q
r
s
t
u
v
W w
x
y
z

leapt

wept

stepped

crept   kept   slept
except   overslept

whistle

bristle   gristle   thistle   dismissal

winner

beginner   inner   spinner
dinner   sinner   thinner

briar liar		flyer fryer

wire

choir			higher

fire	mire	umpire
dire	sire	vampire
hire	spire	
inspire	tire	

Did you hear the **vampire choir**?
Their singing was **dire**
and no one will ever **hire** them
again.

They just don't **inspire**.

wise

a b c d e f g h i j k l m n o p q r s t u v **W w** x y z

It's not **wise** to eat too many **pies**.

I **apologize**.

cries	lies	spies	tries
flies	pies	sties	

buys

sighs

wise

eyes

size

apologize	demise	revise
arise	despise	
clockwise	realize	

142

wobble

bobble   gobble
cobble   hobble

squabble

annual   oval
journal   special

label   trowel
travel   vessel

full
pull

wool

thankful   wonderful
truthful

multiple   stable
muscle   steeple
pimple

a
b
c
d
e
f
g
h
i
j
k
l
m
n
o
p
q
r
s
t
u
v
W w
x
y
z

a
b
c
d
e
f
g
h
i
j
k
l
m
n
o
p
q
r
s
t
u
v
w
X x
y
z

Xx

duvet	**x-ray**	weigh
		obey

Monday	Friday	away	hurray	spray
Tuesday	Saturday	bay	may	stay
Wednesday	Sunday	day	play	stray
Thursday		hay	say	today

Hurray, it's **Saturday**, **stay** under the **duvet** all **day today**.

Come out and **play**.

Go **away**!

Y y

yawn

dawn	lawn	prawn
drawn	leprechaun	spawn
fawn	pawn	

Top of the **morn** to you!

Did you see the **leprechaun** on the **lawn** disappear at **dawn**?

a
b
c
d
e
f
g
h
i
j
k
l
m
n
o
p
q
r
s
t
u
v
w
x
Y y
z

yelp

help   kelp

YELP!
It's the **help**!

Zz

zip

battleship	lip	skip
blip	microchip	slip
dip	nip	strip
drip	pip	tip
flip	quip	trip
grip	rip	tulip
hip	sip	whip

a
b
c
d
e
f
g
h
i
j
k
l
m
n
o
p
q
r
s
t
u
v
w
x
y
Z z

blue   true

horseshoe   shoe

two

zoo

to

haiku

bamboo   kangaroo
boo-hoo   too

blew   threw
grew   unscrew
screw

I tell **you**, a **kangaroo**
wrote a **haiku** at London **Zoo**,
but he **threw** it away,
wrote another next day,
maybe **you** can write **haiku too**!

It's **true**!

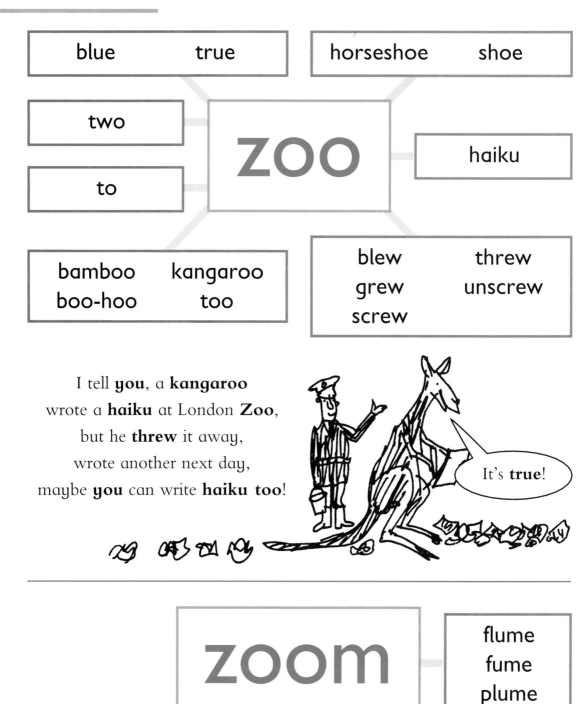

zoom

flume
fume
plume

bloom   bridegroom   gloom   room
boom   doom   loom   vroom

Activities

Activity 1

Play this game with four or more of your friends.

1. Choose one person to start. They should think of a simple start word, for example, *tree*.

2. Each player in turn says a word which rhymes with the start word, for example, *knee, sea, three*.

3. If a player says a compound or multisyllabic rhyming word, for example, *disagree*, he or she can choose a new start word.

4. Any player who can't think of a rhyming word is out.

5. The winner is the player who is left in at the end of the game.

Activities

Activity 2

Write new rhyming lines to complete each of these popular songs and rhymes.

1. Happy birthday to you,
   Happy birthday to you …

2. Hickory, dickory dock,
   The mouse ran up the clock …

3. One, two,
   Buckle my shoe.
   Three, four …

Activity 3

1. Find these words in the A–Z Index on page 160.

   fog   wriggle   purse   craze   proof   brim

2. Turn to the right page to find the rhyming words for each word.

3. Write a short poem for each word using some of the rhyming words.

Example

1. The A–Z Index tells you that *fog* is on page 41 of the dictionary.

2. Turning to page 41, the rhyming words for *fog* are:

dog			dialogue

bog	hedgehog
catalog	jog
cog	log
flog	slog
frog	smog

3. Here is the beginning of a poem using some of the rhyming words:

   When a **dog** and a **frog**
   got lost in the **fog** ...

Activities

Activity 4

Write a jingle to advertise this product.

 Look at page 148 to find words that rhyme with *zoom* and page 44 for words that rhyme with *drink*.

Activity 5

1. Find the headword *hare* in this dictionary.

2. Find another word which sounds the same but which is spelled differently. Words like this are called homophones. Here are some more examples.

earn	urn
hare	hair
peak	peek

Now try to find homophones for these words.

ball	line	berry	rose	boy	waist
find	horse	flower	pen	lock	one

Activity 6

Complete these rhymes.

1. Jello wobbles; ice cream dribbles …

2. Clare McFlare had wonderful hair …

3. Robert's rabbit played the trumpet …

4. When Gran went to the moon …

5. If you want some advice
   When you slide on the ice …

Activities

Activity 7

Add three more lines to this line to write a funny birthday card message to a friend.

I thought I'd send this birthday card…

 Look at page 61 to find words that rhyme with *card.*

Activity 8

Write out these lines of poetry and say whether they are rhyming couplets or rhyming triplets and whether they have internal rhymes.

 Look in the Introduction if you need a reminder.

a. We're stuck up a tree one Sunday in June
hoping that someone comes past very soon.

b. He dazzles spectators with his fancy passes,
don't stare at him without wearing sunglasses,
all other players his skill surpasses…

c. So out I crept behind the shed
then slid on my belly, crocodile style
while my target eyeballed the pond.

d. Look at us now, we're stuck up a tree,
Me, my big sister, and Kevin who's three…

e. Once upon a faraway time
Before the clocks had learned to chime
When every river spoke in rhyme…

Activities

Activity 9

Read the limerick "There was a young man of Kildare" on page 7 of the Introduction. Try to write a different version of this limerick. Begin your poem with the same first line:

There was a young man of Kildare

Remember that a limerick has five lines:

- lines 1, 2, and 5 rhyme
- lines 3 and 4 rhyme.

And your limerick should be funny too!

 Look at page 64 to find words that rhyme with *Kildare*.

Activity 10

1. On page 8 of the Introduction is the rap:

   Matthew, Mark, Luke and Paul,
   drive their teacher up the wall.

2. Read the rap aloud, and clap out a steady rhythm as you read.

3. Read the other two raps on that page, clapping out the rhythm again.

4. Now choose four people you know and write their names down.

5. Read their names aloud and clap out a steady rhythm.

6. When you have got the beat fixed in your mind, write some rhyming lines to create a rap.

Activities

Activity 11

Write a poem about a bee with alternate lines that rhyme. Make it as funny as you can. Then draw a comical picture or a border to illustrate your poem.

 Look on page 23 to find words that rhyme with *bee*.

Activity 12

Read this verse.

Five fat firemen
like fried fish on a Friday.
So five fat firemen
say "Friday is Fry-day!"

If two or more words begin with the same letter like this it's called alliteration.

Look at the pictures opposite. Write a poem that uses alliteration. Look carefully at the pictures before you start and make a list of things that begin with the same letter.

A–Z Index

Cc

163

Ee

Ff

Oo

Pp

Qq

181

Uu

Vv

Rhyming Sounds Index

sound	headword	page number	more rhyming sounds
-able	table	124	-abel
-ace	face	50	-aice, -ase
-ach	match	87	-atch
-ack	back	20	-ac, -ak
-ad	dad	39	add
-ade	shade	120	-aid, -ayed, -eyed
-aft	raft	110	-aughed, -aught
-ag	flag	55	
-age	cage	30	-eige
-ail	nail	91	-ale, -eil
-ain	train	129	-ane, -eign, -ein
-aint	paint	99	
-airy	fairy	51	-ary
-aist	waist	138	-aced, -ased, -aste
-ake	cake	31	-ache, -aque, -eak
-all	ball	20	-aul, -awl
-am	jam	73	-amb
-ame	name	92	-aim
-amp	lamp	82	
-an	van	136	
-ance	dance	40	
-and	hand	63	-anned

sound	headword	page number	more rhyming sounds
-andle	handle	63	-andal
-ang	bang	22	
-angle	angle	16	
-ank	tank	124	
-ant	ant	17	
-ap	map	86	
-ape	ape	17	
-ar	jar	74	ah, are
-arch	arch	17	
-ard	guard	61	-arred, -uard
-are	hare	64	-air, -ear, -ere
-arf	half	62	-affe, -augh
-ark	park	99	-erk
-arm	arm	17	-alm
-art	art	19	
-arter	quarter	107	-ater, -aughter
-ash	ash	19	
-ashion	fashion	52	-assion, -ation
-ask	mask	87	
-ass	glass	59	
-ast	mast	87	-assed
-at	bat	22	
-ate	plate	103	-aight, -ait, -eight
-atter	matter	88	
-awn	yawn	145	-orn, -ourn
-ay	x-ray	144	-eigh, -et, -ey
-aze	blaze	26	-aize, -ase, -ays
-each	reach	111	-eech
-eak	beak	23	-eek, -ique
-ealth	health	65	
-eam	dream	43	-eem, -eme
-ear	ear	46	-eer, -eir, -ere, -ier
-ease	grease	60	-eace, eece, -ice, -iece
-ease	cheese	32	-eas, -ees, -eese, -eeze, -ese, -eys

sound	headword	page number	more rhyming sounds
-east	feast	52	-eased
-eat	eat	47	-eet, -ete
-eck	neck	92	-eque
-ect	insect	72	
-ed	head	65	-aid, -ead
-edge	edge	48	-ege
-ee	bee	23	-ay, -e, -ea, -ey, -i, -y
-eed	seed	119	-ead, -e'd, -ede
-eef	reef	112	-eaf, -ief
-eel	eel	48	-eal
-een	queen	107	-ean, -ine
-eep	creep	37	-eap
-eeve	sleeve	121	-eave, -eive, eve, -ieve
-eg	peg	100	egg
-elf	elf	49	
-ell	well	139	-el
-elp	yelp	146	
-elt	melt	88	-ealt
-en	pen	101	
-ence	fence	53	-ense
-end	end	49	
-ent	tent	126	-eant
-ept	wept	140	-eapt, -epped
-erb	kerb	78	-urb
-erch	perch	101	-earch, -irch, -urch
-erry	berry	24	-ary, -ery, -ury
-ess	undress	133	-es
-est	vest	136	-essed
-et	vet	137	-eat, -ebt
-ettle	kettle	78	-etal
-ext	next	93	-exed
-ib	rib	112	
-ibble	nibble	93	-ible
-ice	ice	70	-ise
-ich	itch	72	-itch

sound	headword	page number	more rhyming sounds
-ick	brick	29	-ic
-ickle	prickle	106	-ickel
-id	lid	82	-ed
-iddle	riddle	112	
-ide	ride	113	-ied, I'd, -yed
-idge	sausage	118	-age
-ie	pie	100	I, -i, -igh, -y, -ye
-iff	cliff	33	if
-ig	dig	41	
-iggle	giggle	57	
-ike	bike	24	
-ile	tile	127	-ial, I'll, isle, -yle
-ill	ill	71	-il
-ilt	kilt	79	-uilt
-im	limb	83	-imb, -ym, -ymn
-ime	time	128	-imb, I'm, -yme
-imp	limp	83	
-in	pin	102	-ine, inn
-inch	inch	71	
-ind	find	53	-igned, -ined
-ing	king	80	
-inge	hinge	65	
-ink	drink	44	
-inner	winner	140	
-int	mint	89	
-ip	zip	147	
-ipe	pipe	102	-ype
-ird	bird	24	-eard, -erd, -irred, -ord, -urd
-ire	wire	141	-iar, -igher, -ir, -yer, -yre
-irl	girl	58	-earl, -url
-irst	first	54	-orst, -ursed, -urst
-irt	shirt	121	-ert, -urt
-ise	wise	142	eyes, -ies, -ighs, -ize, -uys

sound	headword	page number	more rhyming sounds
-ish	fish	54	
-isp	crisp	38	
-iss	kiss	80	-ice, -is
-ist	twist	132	-issed
-istle	whistle	140	-issal
-it	bit	25	-et
-ite	kite	81	-eight, -ight
-itter	bitter	26	
-ittle	little	84	
-ive	dive	41	
-iver	quiver	109	
-iz	quiz	109	-is, -izz
-oak	oak	95	-oke, -olk
-oast	coast	35	-ost
-oat	boat	27	-ote
-ob	mob	89	
-obble	wobble	143	-abble
-obe	globe	59	
-ock	lock	84	-och
-od	rod	114	-ad, odd
-ode	code	35	-oad, -owed
-oft	loft	84	-aft, -offed, -oughed
-og	dog	41	-ogue
-oil	oil	97	-oyal
-oint	point	104	
-old	cold	36	-olled, -ould, -owled
-ole	pole	104	-oal, -oll, -oul, -owl
-olt	bolt	28	-alt, -oult
-ome	home	66	-oam, -omb
-on	salmon	117	-one, -un, -on
-ond	pond	105	-and
-ong	oblong	95	
-oo	zoo	148	-ew, -o, -oe, -u, -ue, -wo
-ood	hood	66	-ould
-oof	roof	114	

sound	headword	page number	more rhyming sounds
-ook	hook	67	
-ool	school	118	-ule
-oom	zoom	148	-ume
-oon	moon	89	-ewn, -une
-oop	swoop	123	-oup, -oupe
-oot	root	114	-uit, -ute
-op	chop	33	-ap
-ope	hope	68	-oap
-or	door	42	-aur, -aw, -oar, -oor, -ore, -our
-ord	lord	85	-ard, -aud, -oard, oared, -oured
-ork	walk	138	-alk, -awk
-orm	uniform	134	-arm
-orse	horse	68	-auce, -oarse, -orce, -ource, -ourse
-ort	sport	122	-aught, -aut, -ought
-ose	rose	115	-ews, -oes, -ows, -oze
-oss	cross	38	
-ot	spot	122	-acht, -at
-other	mother	90	
-otion	ocean	96	
-ounce	pounce	105	
-ound	round	116	-owned
-ount	count	36	
-ouse	house	69	
-out	out	98	-oubt, ought
-ove	dove	43	
-ow	cow	36	
-ow	arrow	18	-ew, -o, -oe, oh, -ough
-ower	flower	55	-our
-owl	growl	60	-oul, -owel,
-own	clown	34	-oun
-own	telephone	125	-ewn, -oan, -one
-oy	boy	28	-uoy

sound	headword	page number	more rhyming sounds
-ub	tub	130	
-ubble	bubble	29	-ouble
-uch	hutch	69	-utch
-uck	truck	130	
-uckle	knuckle	81	
-ud	mud	90	-ood
-udge	judge	75	
-uff	rough	116	-ough
-ug	jug	75	ugh
-ull	wool	143	-al, -el, -le, -ul
-um	drum	45	-om, -ome, -umb
-umble	jumble	76	
-ump	jump	76	
-un	one	97	on, -one
-unch	punch	106	
-under	under	133	-onder
-ung	lung	85	-ongue, -oung
-unk	junk	77	-onk
-unt	grunt	61	-ont
-up	syrup	123	
-ur	fur	56	-er, -ere, -ir, -irr, -or, -urr
-urn	turn	131	-earn, -ern
-urse	nurse	94	-earse, -erse, -orse
-us	us	134	-ous, -uss
-use	use	135	ewes, -ews, -iews, -ues
-ush	thrush	127	
-usk	tusk	131	-usc
-ust	crust	38	-ussed
-ut	nut	94	-utt

About the Authors and Illustrator

Brian Moses

I started writing when I was a teenager. I was inspired by the music of the sixties and tried to play the guitar and write songs. When I realized that I wasn't going to become a rock star I put the guitar away and the songs turned into poems.

I was a teacher for 13 years but since 1988 I have spent my time writing and editing poetry books for children and books for teachers. I also visit schools to run writing workshops and perform my poetry. I have been married to Anne for 26 years and we have two daughters, Karen and Linette.

If you would like to read more of my poems look on The Poetry Zone website: www.poetryzone.ndirect.co.uk

Sue Graves

I live with my husband, four children, a grumpy white cat, a scatty black cat and a very old rabbit in a village near the Roman city of Chester. I spend half my time teaching and the other half writing. When I'm not working I like to play badminton with my friends, but we spend more time talking than playing! Best of all, I love to write children's books.

Tim Archbold

I live in Scotland, near the River Tweed. When I'm not working, I like to walk in the hills, or go fishing, or go for a drive. (My car often breaks down, and I have to push it.) I get my ideas for pictures just from watching people and animals.